All Scripture references taken from the KJV of the Holy Bible, unless otherwise indicated.

TIME is of the ESSENCE by Dr. Marlene Miles

Freshwater Press 2023

ISN: 978-1-960150-29-5

Paperback Version

Copyright 2023

All Rights reserved. No part of this book may be reproduced, distributed or transmitted by any means or in any means including photocopying, recording or other electronic or mechanical methods without prior written permission of the publisher except in the case of brief publications or critical reviews.

Time is of the Essence

Freshwater Press

USA

Table of Contents

Time 6
Time Can Be Commanded 10
The Day 14
The Night 21
The Week 23
The Month 26
Too Late 28
Never Arrived 29
Too Early 31
Spiritual Clocks 32
Right On Time 35
Does Anybody Know 37
What Time It Is? 37
Calendars 40
Seasons 43
The Year 48
The Starting Gate 52
God's Calendar 56
Evil Programming 58
On the First 63
Lay Aside Every Weight 72

Where's My Boo? 74

I Would Not Have You Ignorant 77

Minding My Business 79

Commanding the Calendar 80

Dwell in Safety 82

Abundance & Prosperity 84

Dear Reader: 86

In this book, ATP means **_Any Time Period._**

Time

God created great things in the sky, the sun, moon, and stars to mark time for man, so time must be important.

> And God said, "Let there be lights in the expanse of the heavens to separate the day from the night. And let them be for signs and for seasons, and for days and years, (Genesis 1:14 ESV)

I think of all the ways that God teaches us time and timing. He made the moon to mark the seasons; the sun knows it's time for setting, (Psalm 104:19 ESV).

As time moves on, we are ever coming to the end of something and the beginning of something else. One time period ends, and another starts. We are ever leaving an era, season, week, month, epoch and entering a new one.

Time is of the essence, and as we come to the end of a year, for instance, and the beginning of the next, we make physical plans, we make plans mentally for that crossover and we need to make *spiritual* plans for that crossover, as well.

The phrase, **Time is of the essence** is a legal term that means time is material in the completion of a contract, or timely attention to matters is important. In plain talk, *This can't drag on*. As they say, time waits for no man, so we need to be cognizant of time, times, seasons, and eras. Jesus warned us of that so that we don't miss important times, such as Jerusalem missing the time of Her visitation.

Time being of the essence, means that you could be penalized if you don't complete the contract efficiently, that is, you let things drag on. There could be losses or disappointment in that. Unspoken--, time is of the essence when your teacher tells you to turn a paper in by Friday, but you don't. The penalty is an *F*, or a do-over.

When it comes to spiritual things and time, it's similar because you can't let things drag on if you have spiritual tasks to do. You need to complete things on time for the proper outcome. Else, there could be losses, penalties, even dire straits.

God teaches us how to use time, in better ways than tying a string around the finger or wearing a fancy wristwatch to remind us of things we have to do. There are these huge celestial bodies in the sky--, the sun, moon, and stars to remind us of time and times.

Spiritually, if we aren't aware, if man doesn't acknowledge and use time well, it could be used against him.

When speaking of time here, I'm speaking of time in general, not Divine Time, Set Time, or Appointed Time. Those are times appointed by God. In the Old Testament, appointed times were festival days. Habakkuk 2:3 says that the vision will come to pass at the

appointed time. We do not change or attempt to change God's appointed times.

Time Can Be Commanded

Even though time marches on and waits for no man, we also have some authority over it. Time can be commanded as Joshua did. It is more like we command what happens *within a time frame* than telling time to Stop or Go, as Joshua did.

If we ignore time and do not speak to it, that is, speak to what happens between the start and the finish of a thing, we can be at the mercy of Time. Ancestral altars could be speaking. Or we could be at the mercy of the people who know that Time can be commanded and are actually doing it. Often those people are evil and have no mercy, so we need to be very wise in our living and in our spiritual awareness.

Joshua was wise; he commanded Time.

And the sun stood still and the moon stayed until the people had avenged themselves upon their enemies. Is not this written in the book of Jasher? So the sun stood still in the midst of heaven, and haste did not to go down about a whole day. And there was no day like that day before after it that the Lord hearkened into the voice of a man, for the Lord fought for Israel. (Joshua 10:13-14)

The Word says that there was no day like that or since, but I say it depends on the purposes of God and your faith as to if this will happen again, if you ask God.

Job, even in all of his destruction was concerned about Time, that is, what happens within a certain unit of Time.

Hast thou **commanded the morning** since thy days and caused the dayspring to know his place; That it might take hold of the ends of the earth that the wicked might be shaken out of it? (Job 38:12-13)

Of note, both Joshua and Job seemed to have had the same purpose in mind, *to shake the wicked out of the Earth.* Joshua was in the natural in a battle, while Job was speaking spiritually. Therefore, plans, purpose and intent are important to God if you're *commanding* Time.

I personally think that Time, much like Wisdom is a person. I'd say if we are commanding a unit of Time, then Time is standing guard watching over what happens from the beginning of that unit of Time to the end of it. Time will obey the words of your commands, as long as they line up with the Word of God and you are in proper authority, then you can override any evil commands, even those that may have come first.

Who came first? The evil ones who are intent on stealing, killing and destroying and were probably up all night incanting curses into the day, the night, the week, the month, the year, cyclically onto calendars and even into clocks because that's their assignment and that's what they like to do. They like evil.

Since Christians are not concerned about perishing for a lack of knowledge, or they are too lazy, or too complacent, if Evil enchants into the day and there is no answer, unfortunately Evil will stand. The Christian then thinks it's *que sera, sera.* But it wasn't, it isn't, it was that Evil was programmed into the Christian's day. Evil wants to take hold of the ends of the Earth and shake the good out of it.

What are Christians doing?

The Day

Carpe diem is Latin for, *seize the day*. How do you do that? With your words, your prayers.

The day is an element of time, the morning is an element of time that can be commanded. Every period of time, day, week, month and year can be commanded.

We acknowledge time all the time, we say good morning to people, we say good afternoon, good evening and good night. We can get more specific as we declare good into the morning, declare good into the afternoon and the night. And then be sure to define exactly what GOOD is. In so doing you have commanded the morning, day, and night.

By His celestial bodies and in so many other ways, God is saying things to us about time all the time. God talks to us about time, all the time. What are we saying to God? What are we saying to Time? *Anything*?

He made the moon to mark the seasons. The sun knows it's time for setting, (Psalm 34:19)

It seems that everything, even the sun, the moon, the stars, even the animals seem to understand these laws of nature, the order of God, the timing of things, seasons, days, nights.

Everything, even animals seem to understand these laws of nature, the order of God:

> Even the stork in the heavens knows her times, and the turtledove, swallow, and crane keep the time of their coming, but my people know not the rules of the Lord, (Jeremiah 8:7 ESV).

Mankind, what are we doing? Partying? Nothing? Are we just watching Time go by?

God gives Wisdom to the wise, and knowledge to those who have understanding. Are we just watching the days come and the nights come, and then the days come back again, and we watch the sun, the moon and the stars as if they are works of art and we are in a Van Gough immersive? Are they just objects for romance, poetry, and swoon-worthy songs? Of course, they are, but they are alive, they are living.

We need to do something. If we don't command the day, the night and et cetera, we certainly need to counter-command them. If we don't, this could well explain why we have such bad days, weeks and months sometimes. Even bad years. Anyone who watched Covid devastate the world can agree.

I command the day, the morning, every day, first thing, when I wake up or when I'm fully aware that I haven't done it. I must do it. Sometimes I do it at 6:00 PM because according to Genesis that's when the *day* starts. Ideally, it should be done **before** 6:00 AM, before the dawn, before the sun comes up so you can get ahead of any evil incantations that may have happened in the night against you.

Oh, you're friends with everyone, you don't know a single solitary soul that would ever hurt you. There are two problems with that. The first is that you ***don't*** know OF a single solitary soul that would want to hurt you. *That* you don't know they are doing anything against your will, wishes, or best interest is pretty much the game. They don't want you to know. These could be your best friends, buddies, family, co-workers with their own secret agenda—people who are posing as your best friends.

Oh yeah, I've been told that I'm too suspect of people. Every time I've listened to the advice of geniuses who don't know spiritual stuff, I've ended up feeling the burn. Now I'm back to doing what the Word says, Discern every *spirit*. Even my good Baptist Church I grew up in advised us to *govern ourselves accordingly.*

And that would be according to knowledge.

The second problem is people who ***don't even know you*** are enchanting evil against you. *Like whom?* People who like evil, folks who are intent on evil. Immature, evil people who are just "having fun" to see if spells and incantations "work." Another group are people who are bona fide evil and need to capture souls or do more hurt and harm to get promotions in their evil ranks. People like *Mayhem* on TV commercials – that's more real than you think.

There are people who hate that you are successful, good looking, tall, short, married, or have anything that they want. They want your job, your education, your destiny. Yeah, there's *stuff* happening in the Spirit.

Of course, God can do something about it. But did you miss the part in the Bible where there has to be AGREEMENT in the Earth for God to act? That's where CHRISTIANS come in. You have to speak the Word of God to **make the AGREEMENT** contract so God can do good in the Earth and even on your behalf. You or somebody has to be *speaking* it. Are you speaking it or are you waiting for someone else to do it? No wonder you have hit-or-miss days, weeks, months, years.

Before I get off of this subject, I will make it plain that evil enchanters, witches, wizards and the like are AGREEING WITH SATAN. They are agreeing with the second heaven to get evil into the Earth and into your life.

Again, who is AGREEING with our Father who is in the Highest Heaven, the Third Heaven? *You*? THAT'S WHAT YOU'RE HERE FOR. IF YOU'RE NOT DOING THAT, YOU AIN'T DOIN' NOTHIN.'

Even if you're not praying for yourself, Evil could have happened to somebody else. If you're a true intercessor of God, you care if those incantations could have happened against someone you don't know who is **a child of God is** who is incapable, unable, or doesn't know to pray for him or herself in this season.

So, you get up at 6:00 AM, or whenever you get up,--but you don't pray. If you get up and you don't say anything, you don't breathe a word to God, that's the same as being asleep. Nothing changed. You weren't praying or saying anything of value while you were asleep. So, what changed? How will the spiritual or natural world know you're up? OK, so you get up and you praise, and worship. Perfect! That's great because that is praying--, it's praying to music.

Don't say you don't know how to pray, or you don't know what to say; you pray when you sing. It's just that music has assisted your memory to know what words to use.

You have a heart and feelings and desires inside of you, right? Out of the abundance of your heart, words should flow out to God in prayer.

If you don't have a favorite Command the Day prayer, see the Warfare Prayer Channel on YouTube, https://www.youtube.com/watch?v=xSXnH76VKPU&t=3s

The Night

The night is a unit of time, so I command the night, before I go to sleep. I don't always wait until bedtime, sometimes if I'm stuck in traffic and it's 6:00 o'clock pm, I'll pray it. I always have prayers with me, there are prayers on YouTube, on my phone, and of course prayers flow out of the abundance of the heart.

In a traffic jam, you could pray so you don't waste time. Don't pray just to get out of the traffic jam, use that time well because time is of the essence. It is all about time. Life is about Time and timing.

Command the night, at least by midnight because things happen under the cover of night. Make sure you command the night by midnight.

Witches come out anytime, by day they are in your church, in your workplace, and in your grocery stores, but midnight is considered the witching hour. They love midnight to 6:00 AM while many are sleeping. Unsuspecting. Sleeping. Midnight is a favorite time for them to begin their spells, curses, and incantations--, while we're asleep.

I am not saying that those who are up at night are all witches, some people just have night shift jobs, or are just nightbirds.

The Week

You can command the week in pretty much the same way as you command the day or night. Address it. Acknowledge it. You have a calendar with your week's plans on it; pray about what's on your week's schedule. Some know what they will cook for dinner every night, some know what they will wear for the week. SPEAK to the issues already on your calendar. Speak to your to-do's, your meetings, your strategies, your children's and spouse's itineraries.

There are many types of prayers. Talk to God, ask God about your desires for the week. Commanding the week or any unit of time is when you rise up in authority and declare and decree to the enemies of God. We do not boss God around or even think that we can. I've heard people give "testimonies" where they state, *"I told God--."* Whoa! *Really*? We are not the boss of God, but we are the boss of Evil as long as we are in right standing with God and in our proper position and authority.

Speak blessings over these time periods (ATP). Speak what you want to happen. Speak in authority with confidence. Speak peace and Godly outcomes, all to the Glory of God.

Pray for your neighborhood, community, town, city, state, country. Pray for the world and issues that concern it as well as you and your family.

Speak to any carryover issues from last week. Decree and declare. Now, you're a real prayer warrior! This is a chance to set order and speak blessings, success, and health over your life, starting with the upcoming week.

Use this as an opportunity to nullify and negate the evil and potential evil that may be coming at you. You have authority and dominion so command the week.

The Month

Do the same when commanding the month. You can get more specific with prayer books that address this sort of thing. I recommend Anthony O. Akerele's books on commanding the months and the years. https://a.co/d/4PUQEG0 He gets into details about each month. Find the book that coordinates with your birth month. For example, if you got married in that particular month or even if you were conceived in a particular month, there's a book for that. There is Wisdom in his books and also awesome prayer points.

Stand at the beginning, at the gate of each time period--, day, night, week, month and use your authority and speak the **will of**

God as it concerns you instead of just *letting things happen* as if you have no power. God has made us very powerful beings; we are created a little lower than Elohim.

- **Lord, give me the Grace to see what is in the next day, week, month.**
- I shall not die but live to declare the works of the Lord, in Jesus' Name.
- Evil arrows fired against me at the end of every month, backfire. You will not carry over into the next month, in the Name of Jesus.
- Glory killers that are after the glory that God has ordained for my life, die by fire, in Jesus' Name.
- Every power assigned to use me as a sacrifice, die by fire, in Jesus' Name.
- I fire back every witchcraft arrow fired at me every day, week, month, season, and year, in Jesus' Name.

Too Late

Time is of the Essence. Have you ever gotten someplace too late and missed an opportunity? If you arrived to a job interview late, that might disqualify you. If you arrived at the airport too late, the plane may have already boarded or taken off. If you arrived late to the train station, you might miss the train, and so on.

I warn that the adage, *Better late than never*, may not work in spiritual matters, airplane takeoffs, trains leaving stations and emergency medical situations. If the time has passed, it has passed. The only exceptions are if God redeems the time and restores the years.

Never Arrived

In the real world sometimes never arriving equals a forfeit. If the softball team doesn't show for the tournament the game is lost by the team that never arrived. Same goes for Court, except for the mercy of the Judge. Not arriving in time, on time or at all could adversely affect *connections* in the natural.

Spiritually, not arriving at all, your spiritual and divine connections could suffer. Procrastinating is never a good idea. Procrastination is as the sin of rebellion. Don't miss your blessings by procrastinating. Meet your deadlines. Don't miss your deadlines. You may miss blessings, but there is evil in this Earth counting on you to not answer their Evil, not showing up in prayer, praise or worship because of laziness, complacency, or ignorance. But now you know. Remember, witchcraft, which you may or may not believe in, is very powerful if it is unopposed.

You oppose witchcraft in prayer.

Too Early

Prayers and commanding time can never be too early. The problems only arise or persist when you're too late or never arrive at all.

It is never too soon to start praying for any success, any connection, your children's future, your future, future spouse, children, their careers and their future spouses.

It would be too early to try to minister without being *called*, without being anointed, appointed, and out of season.

Prayers transcend space and time, so pray, God hears your prayers, keeps them and answers them all right on time.

Spiritual Clocks

This chapter is not about the big moon-looking wall clock on the wall of your first-grade classroom, or the digital clock on your nightstand. There are spiritual clocks. Time is kept in the Spirit, obviously.

There is only one spiritual clock that will get you to your destiny. However, there are counterfeit clocks that will be thrown at you like marbles on the floor to trip a burglar in **Home Alone.** Here's the list: Clock of vanity. Clock of death. Clock of sorrow. Clock of failure. Clock of man. Clock of problems. Clock of idols. Clock of witchcraft. Clock of *familiar spirits*. Clock of destruction. Clock of poverty. Clock of infirmity. Clock of marine spirits.

Inside the clock of destiny are the following clocks: Ministry. Marriage. Career. Clock of Glory. Clock of Power. Clock of favor. Clock of Mercy. You are guaranteed success following these clocks. There is no Biological Clock, Sarah had a baby at 99 years old.

Even though women are called to be helpmeets we still have our own Destiny Clock, and we must follow it while we "help" our husbands or help any other people whose destiny helpers we are.

Panic, worry, and anxiety are signs that you are following the wrong clock. Nothing works in a life that is timed with the wrong clock. A person can be pulled in many different directions and following what others say to do (human-driven life). They could be chasing situations, circumstances, or problems. They could constantly be trying to get out of enemy-created problems in life. They could be following their own intellect or what feels right to them.

The person living the Holy Spirit driven life is following the divine destiny clock for their life. They will be successful.

You need to pray fervently to recover a stolen destiny clock, unearth a buried destiny clock, recover a counterfeit or fake destiny clock. Heal and restore a damaged destiny clock or put a fragmented clock back together.

If there is a Divine clock repair shop in the Spirit, we need to find it, and get in it with our prayers and determination. Uncover a covered destiny clock if there is a covering cast over it. If it's been destroyed, we have to ask the Lord to put it back together, gather the pieces, restore the years and redeem the time. ...

- Evil Clocks, stop! Seize and freeze and never work against me again, in the Name of Jesus.

A favorite book, **The Battle for the Clock of Your Destiny** by Tunji Adepoju for more on these clocks. (A most awesome book.)

Right On Time

Right on time prayers are prayed by those who are discerning. They discern the times like the Sons of Issachar, and they also discern *spirits*. They know the times and the seasons of God--, when it's time to sow, reap and harvest. They know the hour of the Lord's visitation. They do not procrastinate.

They know their God and they do exploits. They know all this by Wisdom and by Faith and all that is very pleasing to the LORD.

When Time is of the essence there are certain things that we should be doing at certain times for our advantage, protection and blessings. If we are remiss in doing those things, we could miss out.

We should be commanding every month. Every day, every week, and of course, the year.

These are not one-time prayers; pray without ceasing. Be instant in prayer. *This is the day that the Lord has made, and I will rejoice and be glad in it.*

We will command the week. We are firmly stating to Evil what will and will not be in our upcoming weeks, months, and year. We do this EACH week, each month, each season, and at the beginning of a new year.

We are not commanding God; we are speaking against evil that may be on evil calendars as we have authority to do. Also, God expects us to do this to make Heaven and Earth AGREE so He can work on our behalf.

Does Anybody Know What Time It Is?

Jesus scolded man, He said, ***In the morning, you say it'll be foul weather today, for the sky is red and lowering. Oh you hypocrites can you discern the face of the sky, but you cannot discern the signs of the times.***

Jesus was talking about **His** actual presence on Earth. You have to know what to do and when. Know your seasons of preparation, to be ready when you have to act. For example, you must build up your spirit, man, while it is day, because the night comes when you're resting your soul, you are slumbering and slobbering, and the spirit man needs to be fully charged up.

Jesus knew how naturally minded these men were and that they were not spiritually minded, even though they, themselves are spirit. We don't want to be like that.

That Scripture tells me that Jesus expects us to really know what time it is. You may close your eyes for a moment, and then the moment's gone. You have to discern the time, so you don't miss the moments, you don't miss **_your_** moment, your seasons, or your times.

Don't let your moment come when you are frozen in fear because you weren't prayed up or prepared. So, you did nothing. Your moment or season could have happened when you were up to your neck in flesh works.

Or it seems like you only paused for a moment, and years went by. Decades went by. So much time has gone by. Pray you haven't missed your season, your seasons, or *times*.

It's like watching a movie late at night, and you wake up and the TV's watching you. The whole movie is over. If that movie was your destiny, it's gone.

Lord, redeem the time for us.

Calendars

Then there's the evil calendar which Evil uses to outline the days of stealing, killing and destroying. These are the devil's ultimate goals, but he does it using evil human agents in the Earth who attempt and are sometimes successful at diverting destiny, shooting illness and disease arrows at folks, causing sickness, sorrow and death. Other favorite evil arrows are poverty, and accidents.

Christians, stay prayed up. You don't know, except by the Spirit of God what the enemy has planned for your near or distant future and it can all be preset on an evil calendar.

Oh, you say the devil can't do anything to you. Are you sinning? Do you have an evil foundation with unrepented ancestral sin in it?

If these intangibles are ***missing*** in your life and especially on a regular basis, suspect witchcraft manipulation. Peace. Joy. Happiness. Success. Jesus came that we might have life and that more abundantly. If you are not having an abundant life, there's something wrong.

There's your proof. This is why we must command the day, the night, the week, the month, and the year. It is why we must know the seasons; evil programming may have been incorporated into the calendar.

How can you know if you've been sent an evil arrow, if there has been a witchcraft attack? The unsaved man with the guilty conscience who thinks he is mature will accept *responsibility* and never look any deeper to see why what happened to him happened. Witchcraft? He's a self-made man, he doesn't believe in *that*.

Because he *doesn't believe in that* and does not take proper, spiritual action, he could be taken out.

When something odd happens, the Christian who KNOWS he is walking upright before the Lord will search out a matter. Ancestral sin, evil foundation? Witchcraft attack? In so seeking, he will discover the root cause in time enough to pray and defeat the attack and **live**.

Seasons

Kairos means *time* or *season.* More than that, *Kairos* is the perfect moment, a special, opportune time—one seemingly designed just for right now. (For such a time as this.)

God is always teaching us the rhythm of life. Tithing, for instance, and giving gifts teaches us obedience, yes, but it also teaches us to know *seasons*. We'll know when seasons change. We just won't look at the sky and see if it's red and what the weather will be tomorrow. We'll know the full climate, what's happening. And we'll know what season we are in and God will even show us how to be prepared for what's next.

Lord, teach me to know the seasons and discern the times. Teach me to know when to do what in my life so Your hand of blessing is always on us, that Your face is turned toward us.

Father, forgive us, and give us another opportunity that we promise not to waste.

Time is of the essence; you've got to know seasons; you have to know times. You must move in the right season; you have to move in the right time.

The person who discerns the times and the seasons walks in the Spirit, communes with and hears God. They obey instructions from God. In all their ways they acknowledge God, they allow God to direct their paths.

Seasons change for a reason, and they are called *seasons*, to help us be aware of the season.

We should command these times and seasons to our advantage. In the Name of Jesus. I mean, even if nothing more, we should be opening our mouths to declare the glory and the beauty of God's creations. The sun, the moon, the stars--, the whole Earth is filled with His glory, it is filled with majesty and beauty.

Do we do it? Do we even speak of the glory of God's creation? Some of us do. But some are saying little to nothing about it, and in that the devil has found a way to take what we are not appreciating and turn it to **evil**.

Evil has turned all of what God intended for good into just about a science. There are arrows and evil programming coming at Christians and unsuspecting people all the time. Evil has been put on calendars or in clocks, so it renews itself automatically. This is why we need to be up praying and saying and declaring. We should be opening our mouths to undo these incantations before they hit, or to minimize their damage, or to stop them if they hit once they have started. Prevention is so much easier to stop them before they hit if we're spiritually aware.

- **All Evil renewed at the beginning of a new calendar cycle—, fail to renew against me, fail to renew forever and turn against your owner.**
- **Every evil Calendar catch fire and burn in the Name of Jesus**

Even if you're not spiritually aware, if you know what the Word says, if God says do a thing, do that thing because He said so. It's for our protection, it's for our advantage, it's for prosperity. It's for blessings.

- Any season of sickness rising and falling, death, debt, marital delay in my life, be canceled by the Blood of Jesus.

Season of affliction in my life, fade away by fire in the name of Jesus.

I cancel every season of untimely death in the Name of Jesus. Season of greatness manifest in Jesus' Name.

Seasonal programming is real, don't you get allergies every spring or every autumn? what else? Grief. Pain. Depression? Suspect evil programming if all this came on you as an adult --, more than likely it's not just genetic.

Seasons in the Spirit are named based on what a person is going through, they are not spring, summer, fall and winter. A person could be going through a Dry Season, a Season of Joy, Affliction or in a Wilderness. A person could be in a Season of Trials, Tribulation, War and so forth.

According to the season of life – Sarah brought forth Isaac which means *joy* – it must have been a season of joy for her.

The Year

The sun and the moon and the stars have marked another year. Tonight, it is New Year's Eve where I am. Life is about Time & timing so we will command Time to be in our favor to work for us, *not against us*, let's set things in order with declarations and prayers to bless our TIME and times for the entire upcoming year.

Whenever you are reading this, if it is not New Year's Eve, or New Year's Day pray anyway. Our prayers can transcend space and time—we are kind of like God in that way. It can never do you harm to pray a prayer. If you don't need it, it won't hurt you. If you do need it, it **will** hurt you if you have not prayed it.

We will command time tonight to be in our favor, to work for us, not against us. We will set some things in motion, we will set some things in order, with declarations and decrees. In our prayers we will bless our time for the entire year. We will bless the unit of time--, the time between January 1 and December 31, by declaring, decreeing and blessing what happens *within* that unit of time.

Let's say the Lord gives us each 100 or more years to live; according to His purposes, every minute of that 100 years is important, else God wouldn't give it to us. Praying, praising, and worshipping are excellent ways to spend this time. Yeah, there are parties, ball games, dinners out, and vacations to occupy our time, and there is time for all that, but what will it profit you if you are not spiritually sound in your life, undergirded in prayer?

This is especially important since the enemy is trying to manipulate Time to work against us. He would steal time completely if he could.

Sometimes the enemy can steal from us if we are the type to not pray, that is you are spiritually dry. In this case, we will command

January 1st. We should command the first--, the first of the month, and the first week of the month and the year.

We won't just listen to secular music and watch fireworks or watch a faceted ball drop or go around and make pretty colors and prisms on the wall. I did that in 2019 and thought I was having so much fun, but my 2020 was horrible. There was a pandemic, but still I should have commanded the year instead of letting it just be what Evil had programmed.

You don't' think God came up with the New Year's Eve ball, do you? Really, New Year's is a pagan holiday to celebrate the *god* of war, Mars and the sun *god*, Baal. The devil does all this stuff to distract mankind and look how easy it is to distract us. The devil uses these distraction techniques, and they work.

They shouldn't work on us, but they do work. So, while we are distracted, he's taking things from us that we should be receiving and or keeping, but we are looking at the pretty lights and watching that big ball drop. I mean, it's recorded. We can watch it later, right?

The Starting Gate

Saint of God, there is a gate of entry for every month. There's a point of access for Time and space. It's a place where transition happens. There's traffic there, and traffic control. The control is usually an evil strongman (woman) blocking blessings from you by trying to keep you out.

Sometimes the gate is a meeting place. Remember, that the elders, met at the gate, they sat at the gate. At the beginning of the month is the gate of the month; this part is very important. Stay tuned.

The beginning of this year has a gate for this year. At every gate is a requirement for entry. There is a thief who doesn't want to meet the requirement, so he tries to sneak in. He gets in by any means he can. We must come through this gate decently, and in order. The Lord knows we're not a thief, and He will bless us.

- **Warrior angels of God, take authority over the gate of this new day, week, month, and New Year. Bind the evil gatekeeper and take him away to where the Lord Jesus has for him.**

The King of Glory, the Lord Sabaoth, He is coming in; lift up your heads, all you gates; open up for the King of Glory to come in.

I enter into this new day, this new week, this new month, this new year in the name of Jesus and with the Lord Jesus Christ.

Lord, let the sacrifice of Christ take me through the gate of this month, this week, this day, this year, in the name of Jesus, Gate of this week, month, year become my gate of prosperity, become my gate of healing. Become my gate of deliverance and breakthroughs in the name of Jesus.

I command that time period when I control of the gate.

I take you out of the enemy's hand by the power in the Name of Jesus, I take out healing and good health, riches, gifts, prosperity, successes, blessings, that God has commanded for me this month.

I access you now by the Spirit.

I place a demand on the secrets of the month (any time period) and all the blessings the Lord has for me, in the Name of Jesus. I place a demand on the secrets of the day, week, month, year (ATP – any time period).

I also recover all the blessings not accessed or stolen from me last year, last week, last month, by evil, through my ignorance, pride, rebellion, or lack of action. Lord, forgive me.

Everything that has been stolen from me, I claim them now, **sevenfold**.

This year, this month, this week, this day welcomes me, in the Name of Jesus.

Any evil incantations ever made against me for the month, year, week, day, or night, by the authority, in the Name of Jesus, I deprogram all evil programming established against me, my help, my success, my family, my marriage, my children, my ministry, my career, profession, workplace, in the Name of Jesus.

Lord, let every battle for my time be decided in my favor, in the Name of Jesus. Amen.

God's Calendar

God has a calendar for our lives, a scroll as it were. We all need to embrace the scroll of our lives, the time that it is written about us, (Psalm 40:7).

But I trust in you, oh Lord, I say, you are my God. My times are in your hand. Rescue me from the hand of my enemies and from my persecutors. In the name of Jesus. (Psalm 3:1)

Time is of the essence, and God's calendars and clocks put us in the right place at the right time for divine connections to meet our destiny helpers. Always.

God puts us and sends us where He has commanded blessings for us. God's Word will be a lamp into your feet and a light unto your path. He will order your steps and put you in the right place at the right time, if we ask Him.

Know that there are *wasters* and time wasters. They seek to not only waste time and to waste your life, but they want to control your time and control your time clock.

> But my times are in the hand of the Lord.
> (Psalm 31:15)

Lord, my times are in Your hand.

Say that.

Evil Programming

Anyone sending evil into your life might be creative enough and evil enough to program it into a month, or into the year, on every January 1st, for example. They may program it into every December 31st, or into every birthday or anniversary so it *keeps* happening. They have proclaimed something negative or hateful against you, something opposite of what God would have programmed for you and in God's calendar and the scroll for your life.

Or, YOU MAY HAVE DONE it to yourself, with your big fat, unbelieving mouth! It goes something like this: *It always rains on my birthday.* Or *My husband always forgets our anniversary...* need I go on? That is evil programming; maybe it happened once, it doesn't mean it has to happen all the time. Don't do this to yourself, instead command the day!

God wants us to have an expected end and a good life. There's seasonal programming, for example, some people have allergies every spring, or summer or, fall.

Don't you have repeating grief and pain or depression certain times of the year? That evil has been programmed into seasons for you. We need to break all of that by commanding those times, those seasons, those days, the month, the years in the Name of Jesus.

> But I trust in you, O LORD; I say, "You are my God." My times are in your hand; rescue me from the hand of my enemies and from my persecutors! (Psalm 31:14-15 ESV)

Don't sit back and <u>wait</u> for the same evil to befall you season after season, year after year. DO SOMETHING about it. In the natural people get medicine. Spiritually, which is more powerful because addresses the root of the problem, PRAY, bind, stop the evil programming… break it up! Have faith that you can deprogram this in your life instead of only expecting the same outcome.

How do you know that an evil arrow wasn't sent to you in 2005 so you now believe that every Thanksgiving the family will fight at the dinner table? How do you know that you don't now have faith for it? IF you are not commanding the day, that holiday, that Thanksgiving, then you are giving into the Evil that was programmed into it – even if that evil was only *once*.

I cancel every witchcraft calendar of darkness operating in my life, in the name of Jesus. Any day of affliction scheduled for me on any evil calendar, burn, roast to ashes in the name of Jesus.

Every power using the calendar to fire arrows at me, backfire, in Jesus' Name. (Pray this until you feel a release in the Spirit.)

I cancel every evil calendar of hardship sent, in Jesus' Name.

My destiny, my glory, refuse to run on any satanic calendar, in Jesus' Name.

Cyclical afflictions, monthly, weekly demotion, sickness, catch fire, in the Name of Jesus. Fire of God destroy and engulf every evil calendar working against me in, Jesus' Name.

Lord, STOP all evil calendars working against me, in the Name of Jesus.

Dark powers against my life, be destroyed, in Jesus' Name.

Blood of Jesus, blot my name out of every witchcraft calendar.

Terminal illness or death sentence programmed into any satanic calendar against me, be reversed, in Jesus' Name.

Lord, arise and visit all witchcraft incantations with a thunder quake, in Jesus' Name.

Fire of the Holy Spirit, blind the eyes of every monitoring demon spying on me, in Jesus' Name.

Blood of Jesus, save and protect me and my family, in the Name of Jesus.

Every spirit of sorrow or affliction pursuing me, backfire in the Name of Jesus.

Any evil mark of accidents of any kind placed upon my head, be wiped off by the Blood of Jesus.

Any power or wickedness, planning evil against me this week, month, year, _____ (ATP) fall down and die in the Name of Jesus.

Any power following me for evil be buried permanently, in Jesus' Name.

I call TIME! I call an expiration date on curses, and all childhood and foolish oaths, and vows, in the Name of Jesus.

All seasonal afflictions sent from the pit of hell against me, EXPIRE by the Blood of Jesus, in the Name of Jesus.

On the First

As said, evil may have been programmed into your days, weeks, months and/or years, by some human agent of the devil using the sun, the moon, and the stars and other elements of the Earth.

Like gathering harvests, there are blessings in every unit of time that God has blessed us with that we have to go and collect. We collect them with our words. The only problem is there is demonic opposition; that's why we must pray, declare and decree.

One of my brothers would always say, *I'll do it on the first.* We'd ask, The first of what? Then he'd respond, *The first chance I get.*

We are not kidding here, we are talking out the real **first**, the beginning, the one that opens up the time unit, the one that comes at the start. The first fish the Disciples pulled from the sea had a coin in its mouth. The first can be very special. There is power in the first. There's power in the first of many things, and almost everything. There's power.

In the natural people brag about being the first this, that or the other. That's nice. The first is about more than bragging rights. There's a certain *power* in being the first born, the first son; Jesus was the first born of many brethren. There's power in being the first and if we're not trying to harvest or harness the power of the *first*, we could be missing out.

But the enemy knows about the first. The firstborn of a family is usually under attack, especially firstborn males. Look at Jesus.

The world knows this. Have you noticed that what you have for breakfast you want all day? That's what they say. If you eat sweets and carbs for breakfast, you're gonna crave it all day.

They say if you eat junk, you will want junk all day long. But if you eat healthy, you'll have a healthier appetite all day long. There's power in the first; it sets a precedent for your day, your week, month, year. For your life.

So, when the first is coming up. If we say nothing and do nothing, if we just let our firsts go past, Evil is waiting at the door to take the power of the first that we didn't claim.

If you saw a diamond lying on the ground and you were the **first** to see it --, wouldn't you pick it up?

This is the principle that evil is operating on. Overnight, for example, to program the day the way they want the day to be, they aspire to be the *first*. For that reason, they stay up all night chanting. After dawn the program has probably already started. Did you do anything to counter all that evil?

The first has power.

The **only** has even more power. So, did you correct that evil spoken into the sun, moon, stars or Earth? If you didn't *command* the morning, did you counter-command it? The day? The night? The week? The month? The season? The year?

Let's go get the firsts that the Lord has planned for His people.

- Every evil dedication against me and my blessings, I tender the sacrifice of Christ to undo every evil dedication of this day, week, month, or year (ATP).
- I rededicate this month (ATP) to Christ for divine worship, divine favor and divine provision, for breakthrough, for healing, for deliverance and promotion. In the name of Jesus, Amen.

The Tabernacle was set up in the first month, and the tabernacle of God is with man. Lord, let this _____ (ATP) set me up for worship and tabernacling with You. In Your presence is fulness of joy, peace, prosperity and divine health.

Lord, I speak the best things in my life for my marriage and career and business. In the name of the Lord Jesus Christ, Amen.

Every false *god* honored this day, night, week, month, year, season, I do not honor you. I only honor Christ. Lord, let all covenants established and the false names of these time periods based on the *little g gods* that they throw worship to, I disannul all worship garnered by those false deities. My worship is **only** to Christ Jesus.

Lord, Your Word says that he that is last shall be made first, as the enemy has tried to oppress me to make me last, Lord, turn it around and make me first. The enemy has tried to make me the tail; Lord, make me the head. The enemy has tried to suppress me and make me beneath, by Your Spirit, Lord, make me above only this _____ (any time period).

Make me first in the hearts of my divine helpers, in my ministry, in my workplace, against all competitors, and in every success in the name of Jesus.

Blood of Jesus, cry for me, cry me out of every legal battle, out of every debacle, out of every setback, out of every plan of the enemy against me, in the Name of Jesus. I crossover from failure to success in this new day, month, week, year (ATP), in the Name of Jesus.

Lord, embarrass me with good success and divine favor all year (ATP), in the Name of Jesus.

On the first day of the month, Ezra came out of captivity from Babylon. This is the first, or the first of the day, week, month and I proclaim that I am coming out of every captivity assigned to waste my life, every captivity assigned to prolong singleness, or sickness, or poverty in my life, in the Name of Jesus.

Mighty Angels of God, King of Glory, be my deliverer, in the Name of Jesus. Lord, it is the first, or the first of _____ (ATP). Lord, return my captivity, in the Name of Jesus.

Mighty Angels of God, King of Glory, be my deliverer, in the Name of Jesus.

All honor and glory to Your Name, Lord. Any sin that entered my life this _____ year (ATP) be frustrated and come out now, in the Name of Jesus.

Every problem that located me this year, I reject you by force. I fire you in the Name of Jesus. Lose my coordinates, forget my name, lose my location.

Let all satanic activity in my life be terminated now, in the Name of Jesus. Let the agenda of the devil over my life be terminated now, in Jesus' Name.

Every satanic calendar catch fire and burn to ashes, in Jesus' Name.

Every satanic clock--, Seize, Freeze and Explode, in the Name of Jesus.

Every evil altar projecting evil arrows at me randomly, seasonally, or cyclically be destroyed by Thunder Fire, in the Name of Jesus.

Curses placed upon my life expire now and never renew again, in the Name of Jesus.

Any evil covenant hindering my progress, break by fire, in the Name of Jesus.

Holy Ghost fire burn to ashes every evil deposit in my body and in my life, in the Name of Jesus.

I break free from and loose myself from all unfriendly friends this _____ (ATP), in the Name of Jesus.

Any messenger of trouble that is assigned to me in the _____ (ATP) *die,* in the Name of Jesus.

Father, let my enemies' mistakes backfire and destroy them, in the Name of Jesus. Instead, let my enemies' mistakes favor me.

Every evil arrow pointed in my direction return to sender. Turn, face your sender: AIM! FIRE! Fire those evil arrows at your owner, in the Name of Jesus.

Any evil bullet directed towards me backfire, in the Name of Jesus Christ.

Every arrow of death or hell fired against me, turn around, backfire, in the Name of Jesus.

Lay Aside Every Weight

For those who want to be healthier and lose weight and exercise next _____ week, month, year (ATP):

Lord, help me to lay aside every weight and burden and everything that so easily besets us. And in so doing, give me energy to move, and willpower to resist foods and beverages that are not good for me.

Lord, clean my system of defilement and pollution and make my digestion efficient and pain free. Make elimination effortless and painless. Lord, heal my metabolism and make my absorption of nutrients seamless so that I am healthy, energetic and free of all diseases and disorders, in the Name of Jesus.

Recommended: Read my book, **The FAT Demons, Breaking Generational Curses** to understand the spiritual reasons for overeating and eating to distraction.

Where's My Boo?

For those seeking to get married:

Thank You, Lord for giving me a heart to marry.

You are God of covenant, You love covenant. I pray that You light my path and guide my feet, that I'll make divine connections and meet the person that you ordained that I should marry, in the Name of Jesus.

If I've already met that person, let there be no delay in our engagement.

For those who are married, who want to have a family:

I pray for those who desire to start or add to their family this year:

I pray that all things are done decently and in order in the Name of Jesus.

> And so shall you serve the Lord your God, and He will bless you. He will bless your bread and your water, and he will take sickness away from you in the midst of you. And no one shall suffer miscarriage or be barren among you in your land, and I will fulfill the number of your days.
>
> Exodus 23:25-26

So says the Lord in the Name of Jesus.

Lord, cause confusion among all the people who come against me. Make all my enemies turn their backs to me, in the Name of Jesus.

Lord, let me follow You, and as I follow You and walk upright before You, Lord, as long as I'm in covenant with You, Lord, there will be no barrenness among us, in the Name of Jesus.

If my life or marriage is running on a satanic calendar, Lord, separate me from that evil and put me on your divine calendar, in the Name of Jesus.

Lord, let the Earth yield her increase for me this year _____ (ATP), in the Name of Jesus.

This _____ year (ATP) my spouse and I will grow closer together. Lord, shield us from the wiles of any strange woman, any strange man who tries to enter into or break up our union, in the Name of Jesus.

Lord, give us more Wisdom, more discernment and more Grace this day, week, month, year _____ (ATP).

Lord, draw my family, especially the children with Your lovingkindness and cords of Love; protect, preserve, and provide for them, in the Name of Jesus.

I Would Not Have You Ignorant

Students, those who want to start your education or finish your education or get a job. Lord, You said that you wouldn't have us ignorant.

Let the *Spirit of Knowledge* and Wisdom come upon me now in the Name of Jesus, as I start anew, or continue schooling and educational endeavors, whether high school, college, or beyond.

Lord, give me the mind of Christ to understand all things, recall all things, and the Wisdom for the right application of knowledge, in the Name of Jesus.

Lord, thank You that this year I will finish my education, receive a degree or degrees, certificates, diplomas, and even awards and scholarships.

Thank You, Lord, for divine favor and all my studies with my teachers and professors and exams and matriculation.

I plead the Blood of Jesus over my degrees, diplomas and certificates, all awards and scholarships that will be for my use only and to Your glory, and that nothing by any means can exchange it, take it away, steal it, hide it, bury it, hinder it, or manipulate it in any way to make it not useful to me in the name of Jesus.

Thank You, Lord, for divine favor as I interview and seek proper gainful employment that uses my knowledge and skills, all to Your glory.

In the workplace, Lord, thank You for compensation that is more than enough, all sufficient and abundant, all to the praise of Your glory.

Minding My Business

For those who want to start a new business, I proclaim and declare favor and divine connections over you, and divine Wisdom to know what business to engage in.

I pray that destiny helpers will come to assist you, the customers, clientele, and patrons will be a blessing to you as they bless you in your new business and as you bless them by providing services and goods, in the Name of Jesus.

Excellent prayer for business owners can be found on **Warfare Prayer Channel** on Youtube: https://www.youtube.com/watch?v=VKF4OQI86II

Commanding the Calendar

Twelve months from now may seem like a long time but since our God is full of possibilities, we need to take advantage of them, because those 12 months will probably go by quickly, just as the last 12 did.

Walk upright before the Lord. Seek His face, acknowledge Him, let Him direct your paths. For all saved and sanctified, set free, saints of God, those who want some warfare prayers, let's go:

Lord, if my life has been following a Satanic calendar, I disengage from it now, in the Name of Jesus.

Lord, arise and terminate every Egyptian calendar operating in my life, in the Name of Jesus.

Every evil calendar, burn to ashes in the Name of Jesus.

Every evil clock against me, explode, in the Name of Jesus.

Every counterfeit and evil scroll fashioned to confuse or confound me, burn to ashes, in the Name of Jesus.

I once worked for an old businessman who demanded that his first customer of each day MUST be profitable because he believed it set the tone for the entire day. Obviously, he believed in the power of the *first*.

They say whatever you're doing when the New Year rings in is what you'll be doing all year. I don't know if that's an old wives' tale, or if it's a curse uttered by an evil human agent or the devil himself. At any rate, we should all be found ***doing, occupying, praying, worshipping,*** doing something godly and positive when the new day, week, month, season and/or year _____ (ATP) comes in.

Dwell in Safety

Lord, let every plan against me involving any crime, vandalism, terrorism, violence, kidnapping be canceled, in the Name of Jesus. This year I take back everything that has ever been taken from me, in the Name of Jesus.

Amazing Grace. I was lost, but now I'm found. Lord, I go to the lost and found in the Spirit, I claim and take back everything that's been stolen from me by the enemies of God, in the Name of Jesus.

Lord, fill me with power this _____ year (ATP).

Lord, in the Name of Jesus, I close all open doors against danger, harm, accidents, curses in my lineage.

My household will be safe and secure this year in the Name of Jesus, and we will excel in. whatever we set our hands to do this _____year (ATP) and wherever we go in the Name of Jesus.

I claim the Lord's favor and Grace on my life, family, ministry, education and career in the Name of Jesus. Amen.

Abundance & Prosperity

Lord, we claim abundance in all good things in our lives. We claim financial prosperity in the name of Jesus. Nothing missing, nothing broken. We claim the Shalom of God.

This year, let us show forth and be ambassadors of kindness, goodness, peace, faith, love, all the fruit of the Holy Spirit, and we will be all sufficient, abundant, and prosperous enough to share with others, in the Name of Jesus.

Lord, let all the blessings that you have commanded for me come to me, in the Name of Jesus.

Through the mercies of God, we will find help and support in time of need.

Thank You, Lord, for restoration in every area of my life, redeeming the time, restoring the years in the name of Jesus.

I shall suffer no loss this year, no loss of any good thing in the name of Jesus. I shall suffer no loss of any good thing this _____ (ATP) year in the Name of Jesus.

All year (or any time period) everything I set my hands to do shall prosper to fullness in the Name of Jesus.

I command the day, the night, the month, the year, the seasons, Any Time Period—every time period. I take authority in the Name of Jesus to realize success all to the Glory of God.

In this _____ (ATP) I declare, I will rise and shine. I will no longer sit in darkness or remain in the valley in Jesus's name. I will enjoy victory in every area of my life.

Dear Reader:

Thank you for purchasing this book, may it bless you now and as the message gets into your spirit, may it change the way you view and use Time forever.

Be instant in prayer.
Pray without ceasing.
Pray for others.
Command your days, nights, weeks, months and years to the Glory of God.

Dr. Marlene Miles

Cover art from:
Illustration **37246138** © Gordan | Dreamstime.com

Christian books by this author:

AK: Adventures of the Agape Kid

AMONG SOME THIEVES

As My Soul Prospers

Behave

Churchzilla (The Wanna-Be Bride of Christ)

The Coco-So-So Correct Show

Demons Hate Questions

Devil Weapons: *Anger, Unforgiveness & Bitterness*

Do Not Orphan Your Seed

Do Not Work for Money

Don't Refuse Me Lord

The FAT Demons

got Money?

Let Me Have a Dollar's Worth

Living for the NOW of God

Lord, Help My Debt

Lose My Location

Made Perfect In Love

The Man Safari *(Really, I'm Just Looking)*

Marriage Ed., *Rules of Engagement & Marriage*

The Motherboard: *Key to Soul Prosperity*

My Life As A Slave

Name Your Seed

Plantation Souls

The Poor Attitudes of Money

Power Money: Nine Times the Tithe

The Power of Wealth

Seasons of Grief

Seasons of War

SOULS in Captivity

Soul Prosperity: Your Health & Your Wealth

The *spirit* of Poverty

The Throne of Grace, *Courtroom Prayers*

Time Is Of the Essence

Triangular Powers (4 book series)

Warfare Prayer Against Poverty

When the Devourer is Rebuked

The Wilderness Romance

Other Journals & Devotionals by this author:

The Cool of the Day – **Journal** *for times spent with God*

got HEALING? Verses for Life

got HOPE? Verses for Life

got WISDOM? Verses for Life

got GRACE? Verses for Life

got JOY? Verses for Life

got PEACE? Verses for Life

got LOVE? Verses for Life

He Hears Us, Prayer Journal *in 4 different colors*

I Have A Star, **Dream Journal** *in styles for kids, teen, young adult and up.*

I Have A Star, **Guided Prayer Journal***, 2 styles: Boy or Girl*

J'ai une Etoile, Journal des Reves

Let Her Dream, Dream Journal *in multiple colors*

Men Shall Dream, Dream Journal, *(blue or black)*

My Favorite Prayers (in 4 styles)

My Sowing Journal (in three different colors)

Tengo una Estrella, Diario de Sueños

<u>**Illustrated children's books by this author:**</u>

Big Dog (8-book series)

Do Not Say That to Me

Every Apple

Fluff the Clouds

I Love You All Over the World

Imma Dance

The Jump Rope

Kiss the Sun

The Masked Man

Not During a Pandemic

Push the Wind

Tangled Taffy

What If?

Wiggle, Wiggle; Giggle, Giggle

Worry About Yourself

You Did Not Say Goodbye to Me

www.ingramcontent.com/pod-product-compliance
Lightning Source LLC
Chambersburg PA
CBHW070856050426
42453CB00012B/2233